Doing Money God's Way Workbook

Jason & Kristel Finns

Copyright © 2017 Jason & Kristel Finns

All rights reserved.

ISBN-10: 1976276675
ISBN-13: 978-1976276675

Unless otherwise noted, scripture taken from the New King James Version.

Copyright 1982 by Thomas Nelson, Inc.

This workbook supplements our book *Doing Money God's Way: Financially Free for a Purpose* to provide a useful tool for personal finances. However, these materials are distributed with the understanding that neither the authors nor the publisher are providing professional financial, legal, or accounting services.

This workbook was created to make the book of the same name more practical and meaningful. You can work through this study in a group setting or independently. If you are working independently, you might consider inviting a friend, co-worker, or neighbor to join you but it is not necessary. We suggest married couples work through this together if possible. You will realize significantly better results by working together.

INTRODUCTION

Some financial studies start with practical wisdom and then later tie that into what the Bible says. We take a different approach in that we begin with a biblical viewpoint to lay a foundation before delving into practical application. Over time we have seen numerous individuals realize financial breakthrough, marriages become more united, and blessings poured out on those who have walked the path towards financial freedom.

Before moving on, take a few moments to pray over this journey. Ask God to come alongside you to talk to you and guide you in how to glean what you need from this experience.

Father God, we come to You in the name of Jesus. We invite Your Holy Spirit to guide us into truth as we set upon this journey to learn more about how You want us to handle our finances. In Jesus' Name, Amen.

Next Steps:

Respond to the following questions and read Chapters 1 and 2.

**Group Participants: If you are completing this in a group setting, you will need to do this prior to the first group session.

We have watched people start this study and then drop out midway and understand there are many legitimate reasons. Our question to you is, "Why are you determined to complete this study? Why is this important to you?" Write your answer below.

Which item below describes your current view of money?

   a. a necessary evil
   b. a trophy
   c. a point of contention with your spouse/others
   d. a tool God uses to bless you and others through you

You don't have to stay where you are! If at any point you feel guilty or condemned, do not let that stick with you. We pray you find true freedom that only Christ can give you.

Throughout the study, regardless of your current financial situation, keep Roamans 8;1a below in focus:

There is therefore now no condemnation for those who are in Christ Jesus.

SESSION 1
CHAPTERS 1 & 2

Open your study today with prayer. The following verse, taken from Phillippians 3:13, is helpful to use as a guide in your prayer:

Brethren, I do not count myself to have apprehended, but one thing I do, forgetting those things which are behind and reaching forward to those things which are ahead.

Let's get started! We are believing that great things are in store for you!

1. How important is money in determining the kind of TV shows, music, and movies that are commercially supported.?

2. Complete the following: "If Christians continue to approach finances the way the world does... ."

3. How could Christians be more effective if they considered their employment a Kingdom assignment?

4. How does God expanding His Kingdom on the earth relate to how Christians manage money?

5. Paraphrase the verse below and answer the question, "Why do we need God to bless us?"

   God be merciful to us and bless us, and cause His face to shine upon us, ...That Your way may be known on earth, Your salvation among all nations. Psalm 67:1-2

6. Say or read "The Lord's Prayer" in Matthew 6:9-13. How could this apply to us right now during this study of *Doing Money God's Way?*

Next Steps

Before completing the next section, read Chapter 3.

SESSION 2
CHAPTER 3

Note to Group Leaders:

If time allows, divide this chapter study into 2 sessions, stopping after question 4 for the 1st session.

Though this session addresses marriage, certain elements pertain to everyone. Some participants may be married and taking it independently. Others may be single and potentially looking for qualities in a future spouse. Still yet, the money character traits section is a place to identify areas of personal weakness for anyone, married or single.

Begin your lesson with the following prayer and scripture to set the tone

Father God, we come to you in the name of Jesus. Today, as we yield ourselves to Your Holy purpose, we ask You to come and help us. We ask You to walk us through this journey in humility, with a heart to purely love one another and grow in unity. We lay down past experiences and open our hearts to hear You speak to us in a fresh way. We trust in Your Holy Spirit to fill us with wisdom and guide us to all truth in Jesus' Name. Amen.

Accountability is one of the biggest hurdles in managing money together as a married couple. Are you in the habit of referring to money as "his debt" or "her money?" If so, work toward a shared "our money." Mark 10:7-9 reminds us that after we are married, we are one.

"For this reason a man shall leave his father and mother and be joined to his wife, ⁸ and the two shall become one flesh'; so then they are no longer two, but one flesh. ⁹ Therefore what God has joined together, let not man separate."

1. Being open and honest provides freedom, and accountability requires less work in the long run. Read Ephesians 4:25 below. What is Paul telling Christians that can be applied to money and marriage?

    "...Let each of you speak the truth...for we are members of one another."

2. How important is financial honesty in a marriage? In your marriage? Do each of you agree on this point and how to become financially accountable to each other?

3. How do the following characters present themselves in regards to marriage or in individual personalities?

   a. Pinocchio

   b. Wimpy

c. Pip & Squeak

d. Eeyore

e. The Wicked Witch

4. Married Couples: Based on "The Kingdom Couple" section, how do you seek His Kingdom in your marriage?

Stopping point for groups dividing this into 2 sections. This is also a good time for everyone to stop and reflect. This can be heavy to work through. Keep a humble and prayerful heart.

As you begin conversations on your journey to financial freedom, embrace these four tips when addressing money and marriage.

1. Don't nag.

2. Don't dictate.

3. Remember that you can't fix your financial situation all in one night, but you can repair it together.

4. Take time to dream together.

5. Read Genesis 11:1-9 about the Tower of Babel. There is truth that applies to our study on financial freedom.

6. God was disappointed in the people of Babel, but the lesson for today is the power of speaking in unison. Verse 6 reads: *"And the LORD said, "Indeed the people are one and they all have one language, and this is what they begin to do; now nothing that they propose to do will be withheld from them."*

7. What are some ways people might speak negatively over their finances? List some ways a husband and wife might speak the same language with negative effects? One example might be both spouses saying, "We can never get ahead. Things always break when we try to save."

8. What are some ways we can speak positively over our finances? What positive outcome can result when a husband and wife speak the same language in a good way? Questions 9 and 10 will give some tips if you want to look ahead. Warning: speaking God's Word in unison is a force to be reckoned with in any area of our lives! Get ready for great things. Expect the miraculous!

9. Review and discuss the following positive benefits of speaking the same language:

   Understanding God's financial plan for us creates increased unity and overall health of the marriage.

   Speaking God's Word about your situation activates your faith and focuses the attention on God as your provider.

   Speaking positively motivates you to keep pushing through trying times.

   Focusing on a brighter day ahead and changing your outlook on what could otherwise be a desperate situation provides hope and trust in God's provision.

10. Review and discuss the following examples of speaking the same positive messages.

    "God's got this. He's going to bring us through this hard time."

    "I'm excited to see how He's going to work this challenge out."

    "If I don't get this job, I know He will provide another as long as we trust in Him."

In your conversations do not allow the "what ifs" to creep in. Stand firm in your faith as you continue to steward well and work diligently. Now you have the power of the same language to build a tower, which is something of eternal significance, for the Kingdom! How will you begin to do this?

Romans 15:5 is an excellent verse to pray and begin a fresh step toward unity. You can do this by inserting "us" in place of "you." *"Now may the God of patience and comfort grant you to be like-minded toward one another, according to Christ Jesus, ⁶ that you may with one mind and one mouth glorify the God and Father of our Lord Jesus Christ."*

Homework:

1. Take a few minutes and discuss your financial goals. If you are married and both spouses are participating, write two financial goals on which you agree.

Married Couples:

2. Each spouse - write one financial topic/goal upon which you do not agree with your spouse, assuming you do not agree on a financial issue. For example, one spouse thinks the family should save money by not eating out as often, but the other disagrees.

3. Start to pray about the "disagree" list, but don't try to fix it. Start to listen for gentle promptings from the Holy Spirit for the next steps to take. Humility and prayer are two keys to success in this area.

For additional references see: Philippians 4:19, Psalm 37:25, and Malachi 3:10. Write these verses down. Memorize them and pray them over your finances Put your name in the verse to make it personal. Speak aloud what His Word says even if you do not see anything at the time. You are putting your faith into action. His Word will not return void or empty. — Isaiah 55:11.)

Next Steps

Before the next lesson read Chapter 4.

SESSION 3
CHAPTER 4

Note: You will reference the section below throughout this study with a special space for writing goals in Appendix A, located in the back of the workbook.

Begin by praying and asking God to open your heart to what He has to say to you today.

1. Describe the differences between goals and dreams.

2. Are there any areas of your life you have felt hopeless or headed for disaster, specifically in the area of finances? Based on Jeremiah 29:11 below, what does God's Word say about your situation?

For I know the thoughts that I think toward you, says the LORD, thoughts of peace and not of evil, to give you a future and a hope.

"Goals teach us discipline while dreams reveal our destiny." Prayerfully take some time to ask God to reveal His dreams for you. It is ok if they do not sound all that spiritual. These dreams might be the very thing God uses to take you to your destiny.

Consider Proverbs 29:18, which says, *"Where there is no vision, the people perish...."* (KJV) Then to get you started, take a look at these points. Sometimes the answers to these questions can reveal much about our destiny.

To help identify your dream/destiny, ask yourself:

What angers me?

What excites me?

What makes me sad?

3. What would you do if money were no object? Ok, try to think deeper than just laying on a beach on your own private island for the rest of your life!

Take some time before the next session to write down your goals and dreams in the special page dedicated for this purpose in Appendix A. You might even want to share some of goals and dreams with someone else!

Don't be discouraged if you can't nail down your goals and dreams today. This will likely be a process that develops over time. Flag the goals and dreams page and keep coming back to it, asking God to speak to you on this topic.

Next Steps

Read Chapter 5 before the next lesson.

SESSION 4
CHAPTER 5

Begin this session by taking a moment to meditate in prayer on where you are in your journey to financial freedom. What can you be thankful for today? What praises do you have to offer? Ask God to open your heart to hear Him speaking to you starting today.

1. Review the opening statement of Chapter 5 and finish the following sentence. "Learning how to steward or manage money well is critical to…"

2. What are the budgeting lessons for each of the following scriptures?

   "Go to the ant, you sluggard; consider her ways and be wise, which, having no captain, overseer or ruler, provides her supplies in the summer, and gathers her food in the harvest." Proverbs 6:6-8

"Prepare your outside work, make it fit for yourself in the field; And afterward build your house." Proverbs 24:27

"Be diligent to know the state of your flocks, and attend to your herds;" Proverbs 27:23

For which of you, intending to build a tower, does not sit down first and count the cost, whether he has enough to finish it lest, after he has laid the foundation, and is not able to finish, all who see it begin to mock him, saying, 'This man began to build and was not able to finish?" Luke 14:28-30

3. How do you "get the big rocks in first" when budgeting?

4. Complete this sentence. Most of money management is…

5. What should you do for the next 30 days if you aren't living on a budget right now?

6. Complete the following exercise using the "Zero-Based Budgeting" section.

   Pay _____ first.

   Pay _____ second.

7. What determines how much is paid in the second line item?

8. What is meant by zero-based budgeting?

9. Your first budget will _____!

Homework #1: Select a set time for your money date. You will most likely need about an hour. Write it here:_____

If you are married, set a time and location that suits both spouses. Both need to participate in some way even if one is leading and the other is there to discuss updates or changes that need to happen to meet budget for the month. If you are married and your spouse is not ready to participate, create your own money date with hopes of a joint money date in the future. This does not have to be a large amount of time. The goal is that it becomes an increasingly shorter amount of time so your time can be spent on other things.

Writing this date generates great power. Put your money date in your calendar. Set an alarm to go off on your phone. Tell someone. Make a banner for your wall, rent a billboard — you get the idea! Stick to your appointment, and don't let a week go by without having your money date. Create a money date for yourself if you are single. If you do get off track just jump right back to this key element to staying on a budget. This action will keep you on target and make corrections easier if you are tracking each week.

Homework #2: Use your money date to track all expenses for the next 30 days. Do not make a budget yet. Just track spending so you will know how to set your budget if you haven't previously made one .

Homework #3: Pick a money date that occurs at least 30 days from now during which you will create your first budget. Put it in your calendar with an alarm!

Next Steps

For the next lesson you, will need to read Chapters 6 and 7.

SESSION 5
CHAPTERS 6 & 7

Open in prayer and thanksgiving. Can you find at least one specific praise you have experienced thus far since beginning the study? What specific prayer do you have in regards to the study today? We encourage you to share your praises and prayers with someone else if possible.

An encouraging reminder in Philippians 4:13 is probably a verse you have heard often. *"I can do all things through Christ who strengthens me."*

1. Reread Proverbs 22:7. What does the Bible tell us about borrowing?

2. True or False? When buying a car it is better to buy a new one.

3. What are the dangers of keeping a credit card for reward points? What if you pay it off every month?

4. What does it mean to "flip the debt switch"?

5. When paying the mortgage, we can pay extra as we have it and ask God to help us by meeting us where we are. He is able to give us a debt-free house! Add to your "Dream" page (in the Appendix) what you would do if you did not have a mortgage payment.

6. We often let "just enough become the enemy of ... ."

7. How does having an emergency fund impact our budget when unforeseen expenditures occur?

8. Savings must be intentional. What are your action steps to an emergency fund if you do not have one?

9. Where should you keep your Emergency Fund?

   _____

10. How much should you plan to save for an Emergency Fund, according to most financial experts?

11. What are the 3 strategies for addressing unplanned financial emergencies?

Homework: If you have debts, create a debt snowball. The debt snowball is a fast technique for deciding the order to pay off debts. You can do a quick Internet search to easily learn more on this topic. We have included a special page in the Appendix to record your debt snowball so you can easily refer to it in the future.

Now is a great time to revisit the Goals and Dreams section that you completed in Session 3. Keep revisiting as you go throughout the study. "If you aim at nothing you will hit it every time." — Zig Ziglar

Next Steps

For the next session, read Chapter 8.

SESSION 6
CHAPTER 8

Open in prayer before beginning. Are there any financial struggles do you need to take before the Lord today? Be encouraged that He is the God of more than enough.

"Buy my God shall supply all your need according to His riches in glory by Christ Jesus." Philippians 4:19

Read Matthew 25:14-30.

1. What are the main lessons from the parable of the talents?

2. Describe the principle of stewardship.

3. What should come before investing?

4. What are the benefits of mutual funds compared with individual stocks?

5. Complete the following regarding the 10-10-1 Rule.

   Pick mutual funds that are at least _____ years old.

   Look for an average return of at least _____% since inception.

   Never pay more than a _____% in expenses.

   Never pay load fees! Load fees are fees paid to purchase or sell mutual funds.

6. What is a simple definition of diversification as it relates to investing?

7. What is the "smile and wave" principle?

Homework: Focus on speaking and thinking good things over your financial situation. Married participants: Remind yourself what it means to "speak the same language" and continue to work towards unity in your two agreed upon financial goals.

Next Steps

Before the next session read Chapters 9 and 10.

SESSION 7
CHAPTERS 9 & 10

Open in prayer and review Psalm 92:12-15 below. Proclaim what God's Word says about us as believers. Insert your name within the scripture.

"The righteous shall flourish like a palm tree, He shall grow like a cedar in Lebanon. Those who are planted in the house of the LORD Shall flourish in the courts of our God. They shall still bear fruit in old age; they shall be fresh and flourishing. To declare that the LORD is upright; He is my rock, and there is no unrighteousness in Him."

1. What is a free agent in God's Kingdom?

2. In general, you should have _____ times your ending salary saved for retirement.

3. An ideal target for retirement savings each month is _____ of your income.

4. Retirement Fund Mechanics

   First, contribute up to the employer's match in the _____. Then save in a _____ until you reach the savings goal of 15% or until you hit the maximum contribution. If you are able to save more, you can resume saving in the _____.

5. Complete the following. "Social Security was never meant to be a … ."

Note: Never cash out retirement early unless it is to avoid bankruptcy.

6. What must be coupled with stewardship to see measurable results in financial freedom?

7. What is the difference between fact and truth? On which do we need to focus?

8. What role do our words play in our finances and every area of our lives?

Action Items:

1. Remember to keep receipts for EVERY purchase in a designated place.

2. Are you keeping your weekly money date? Stay at it! You will reap a harvest if you do not give up! Invite the Holy Spirit into your finances and watch Him show up in BIG ways!

Next Steps

Before the next session read Chapters 11 and 12.

SESSION 8
CHAPTERS 11 & 12

Open in prayer.

1. What is the key to truly understanding finances from a Kingdom perspective?

2. What happens when we seek more money just for the sake of having more money?

3. Is it OK to enjoy the benefits of having money? Read Psalm 35:27, Proverbs 21:20a, and 1 Timothy 6:17 before answering.

4. While looking at Psalm 23:5, how can we relate our cup running over to our finances? Is it OK to want just enough to provide for yourself? Is desiring more wrong?

5. What has He promised in Malachi 3:8-12 to those who pay tithes and give offerings? When we fail to give back to God in tithes and offerings, in what ways have we restricted ourselves?

You might find printing the above verses from Malachi 3:8-12 and putting them where you will see them helpful. Then you can remember to apply these promises to your prayers over your finances as you pay bills at your weekly money date.

6. What percentage of Christians regularly tithed when *Doing Money God's Way* was published?

7. How could praying over your tithes and offerings benefit you and what verses would be beneficial as you pray? Write them below.

8. When we sow seed, also known as giving, does it always produce an immediate harvest (a return back to you as promised in scripture)? How can we apply the concept of seed, time, and harvest to our giving?

9. What does "Don't eat your seed, and don't sow your bread" mean?

10. Giving to _____ and not to _____ will change the way you give.

11. In closing, with all the principles we've learned, we must all answer one question that matters more than anything. What is that question? What is your answer? If you want to discuss your answer, speak with your group leader or a pastor.

DOING MONEY GOD'S WAY
DECLARATION OF INDEPENDENCE

We sow financially into God's Kingdom because we believe His Word and live by our giving.

We honorably steward what God has given us by living on less than we make and meticulously budgeting the rest.

We save not to lay up treasure on earth but to provide a foundation for living that enables us to more effectively build the Kingdom according to Proverbs 21:20.

We use cash because we do not need the world's credit.

We invest for retirement in order to make more of what God has blessed us with according to Matthew 25:14-30.

We pay off our houses because we believe money is better spent on financial principles than paying interest to the world.

We have broken our dependence on the world's system of handling money because we believe God's way is better.

CONCLUSION

Thank you for joining us on this journey! Our hearts' desire is that *Doing Money God's Way* has been a blessing to you and will impact not only you but the lives of the many YOU are called to reach. Others are waiting for what YOU are called by God to offer. Freedom awaits! His plans for you are great!

Be diligent to stay the course. Work hard. **Pray and trust** in the One who is faithful. **Stay committed** to see this journey to financial freedom through to something beautiful, *not just for you but for others.*

"The flowers of tomorrow are in the seeds of today." Author Unknown

All the Best,

Jason and Kristel

We would really love to hear your stories of financial freedom. Even small successes are a big deal! We would love to help you celebrate!

Here's how you can reach us:

Facebook: Doing Money God's Way

Our website: www.doingmoneygodsway.com

Email: doingmoneygodsway@gmail.com

APPENDIX A
GOALS & DREAMS

"Where there is no vision, people perish." — Proverbs 29:18 -KJV

Ponder this:

Where there is no vision… unity in marriage is divided.

Where there is no vision… budgets aren't executed.

Where there is no vision… debt isn't addressed.

Where there is no vision… savings goals aren't met.

Goals

Dreams

APPENDIX B – BUDGET TEMPLATE

Permission is granted to copy this page for your own personal use.

Budget Template

Income	Budget	Weeks					
		1	2	Total	3	Total	4
Tithe (from gross)							
Debt Reduction							
Groceries/Household							
Mortgage							
Utilities							
Gasoline							
Large Expenses (See Appendix B in book)							
Insurance (if paid monthly)							
Phone/Cable/Internet							
Husband's Entertainment							
Wife's Entertainment							
Eating Out							
Miscellaneous							
TOTAL							

APPENDIX C
DEBT SNOWBALL

Jason & Kristel Finns

www.ingramcontent.com/pod-product-compliance
Lightning Source LLC
Chambersburg PA
CBHW062159220526
45470CB00009B/2868